Elegant Software
Design Principles

Narayanan Jayaratchagan

Contents

Dedication

I dedicate this book to my grandparents, Lakshmi and Thiruvengadaramanujadasar.

Acknowledgements

I would like to thank the following for their ideas, help, review and encouragement: Rajnarayanan Kannan, Balachandran AV, Sankarasubramanian K, Job Samuel, Sasikumar Pallekonda, Siddharth T, Rajendran R, Ganapathy Subramanian Natesan , Vijayanantha Ganesh and N M Hussain.

Special thanks to my wife Bobbypriya, daughters Lakshmi and Vaishnavi for their support.

Feedback

I would love to get your feedback. If you have questions or suggestions or corrections, please use the feedback/errata submission form - https://goo.gl/forms/e0bU0g9kUt1Olqzw1.

Introduction

This book is based on a simple but powerful observation: professionals who design and develop elegant software do so primarily by mastering a set of important related principles - fundamental ideas, which they use repeatedly. This naturally leads to the question - what are those recurring principles? Within these pages are 50 principles for your reference to help you design elegant software.

Elegant Software

How do we know whether the design of a software under consideration is elegant or not? There are two different ways to measure the quality of software design:

- Quality Attributes Driven Approach and
- Design and Code Smells Driven Approach

In practice, we usually end up with a combination of these two approaches to assess the quality of the design along with a set of design metrics.

Quality attributes approach drives the measurement through analysis of how well the design supports the following properties:

- Usability – is it easy for the client to use?
- Completeness – does it satisfy all the client's needs?
- Robustness – will it deal with unusual situations gracefully and avoid crashing?
- Efficiency – will it perform the necessary computations in reasonable amount of time using reasonable memory and other resources?
- Scalability – will it still perform correctly and efficiently when the problems grow in size by several orders of magnitude?
- Readability – is it easy for another programmer to read and understand the design and code?
- Reusability – can it be reused in completely different setting?
- Simplicity – is the design and/or implementation unnecessarily complex?
- Maintainability – can defects be found and fixed easily without adding new defects?
- Extensibility – can it be easily enhanced by adding new features or removing old features without breaking code?
- Security – is the s/w protected against known security vulnerabilities?
- Testability – is it easy to test the components using automated unit tests?

Design and code smells approach drives the measurement through analysis of the design for symptoms or smells like the following:

- Rigidity – Changing the design is difficult
- Fragility – It's easy to break
- Immobility – Reuse is difficult
- Viscosity – Doing the right thing is difficult
- Needless complexity – Over engineered design
- Needless repetition – Copy paste reuse
- Opacity – Incomprehensible design

Presence any of these smells indicate poor design and they are often caused by the violation of one or more design principles. Design principles play a significant role in both the approaches:

- Applying the design principles appropriately helps to achieve these desired qualities.
- Applying the design principles appropriately eliminates the design smells and lead to good design.

Design Pyramid

There are many ways to organise the literature and wisdom related to software design and development. The design pyramid is my attempt to describe the conceptual framework for mastering the design and programming skills required to develop elegant software. The design pyramid has three faces. I refer to them as Familiar Face – Tactical Knowledge, Ideal Face

– Strategic Knowledge and Real Face – Practical Knowledge.

The Familiar Face – Tactical Knowledge

It is quite common among the software developers to identify themselves with the programming language they are familiar with. For example, I used to refer myself as a Java developer in the early stages of my career and used to think of software design and programming using the constructs offered by the Java programming language, libraries and frameworks like Spring and Hibernate to name a few. Experience with preferred tools like Eclipse, Maven, etc are often included as part of the job descriptions. Reference implementations published by vendors act as the gold standard developing applications using the specific platforms like JEE and .Net. I refer to this as tactical knowledge because most of these are commodity skills. This familiar face representing the tactical knowledge is depicted below.

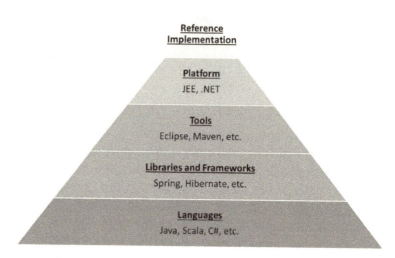

Design Pyramid - Familiar Face – Tactical Knowledge

The Ideal Face – Strategic Knowledge

It's perfectly fine for a developer to start with the familiar face – tactical knowledge, but the problem with it is, it limits the individual to a specific language and platform. In the current world of polyglot programming, working with multiple languages is the norm. The best thing one can do to keep their knowledge and skills portable is, to make conscious effort to learn the underlying principles, patterns and practices that are universal and promote development of elegant software. The ideal face – strategic knowledge of the design pyramid is depicted below.

Design Pyramid - Ideal Face – Strategic Knowledge

The Real Face – Practical Knowledge

Everyone wants to design and develop elegant software but we end up with software that is not so elegant and riddled with smells and antipatterns. It's important to know what rots the software and how to avoid or fix them. Refactoring and Continuous inspection of the code we develop help us to do the necessary course correction required to eliminate the smells and antipatterns to make the software more elegant. The real face of the design pyramid is depicted below.

Design Pyramid - Real Face – Practical Knowledge

Principles Catalogue

This book focuses primarily on documenting the core elements - design principles and practices that constitute the foundation for the Strategic Knowledge – Ideal Face of the design pyramid along with references to elements of the Tactical Knowledge - Familiar and the Practical Knowledge - Real faces as applicable to the context.

This book features 50 key principles essential to design elegant software. These principles are logically grouped as in to the following sections:

I.   The Driving Principles - describes the three most important principles that drive almost all design decisions

II.   Core Principles - describes the fundamental principles all developers should be familiar with

III. SOLID Principles - describes the five principles which could be considered the corner stones of elegant design

IV.   GRASP - describes a set of principles which provide guidance on assigning responsibilities to classes

V.   Reliability Principles - describes a set of principles that lead to highly reliable systems

VI.   Package Design Principles - describes a set of principles to help group classes in to packages

VII. General Principles - describes the rest of the essential principles

Principle Documentation Template

I use the following template to describe the principles documented in this book.

Name of the Principle - Well-known name of the principle.

Also Known As - Other names of the principle.

Original Contributors - Individuals who originally coined the principle and/or made significant contributions to its literature. I've used *Community Wisdom* when a principle could not be attributed to specific individual(s).

Principle - the principle statement.

Explanation - Brief description including the motivation and other aspects behind the principle.

Quality Attributes Affected - lists the quality attributes the principle caters to.

Metrics - lists applicable metrics if any to measure the quality of the design objectively.

Smells - lists design and/or code smells which could be eliminated through applying the principle.

See Also - lists the set of related principles.

The Driving Principles

In the early 1970s, Larry Constantine questioned the meaning of "good design". He proposed several new notions of design structures that could help designers to evaluate design quality. This section covers principles catering to three of the most important design concepts:

- Complexity
- Cohesion
- Coupling

The main purpose of modelling and design before doing the development (coding) is to be able to **manage the complexity** of the system under development.

Highly cohesive and loosely coupled design is the ultimate objective.

Manage Complexity (MAC)

Also Known As: Simplicity

Original Contributors: Fredrick P. Brooks, Jr. Thomas J. McCabe, Sr., Maurice Howard Halstead, Larry Constantine, George Miller

> Minimize accidental complexity and manage essential complexity.

Complexity is a measure of the interactions of various program elements. It is a direct indicator of quality and costs. Specifically, if the complexity of code is high, the quality of that code will be lower and it will cost more to manage it.

The need to reduce complexity is mainly driven by limited ability of people to hold complex structures and information in our working memories. Frederick Brooks classified complexity into two types: essential complexity and accidental complexity. Essential complexity is the inherent complexity of the problem to be solved. Accidental complexity is all the problems created by the developer as part of the design and development of the solution.

Essential complexity cannot be eliminated but managed through properly applying many of the design principles like Abstraction, Separation of Concerns, Modularity etc.

Accidental complexity can be minimized or eliminated through emphasizing the creation of code that is simple and readable rather than clever. Making use of standards and following clean coding practices helps to minimize accidental complexity.

Quality Attributes Affected

Improves: Testability, and Maintainability

Reduces: Complexity, and Coupling

Metrics

Cyclomatic Complexity, Halstead Metrics, Coupling Metrics, Connascence, Lines of Code, Interface Complexity and Maintainability Index.

Smells

Spaghetti Code, God Class, Proliferation of Classes, Duplicated Code, Contrived Complexity, Large Class, Large Method, Feature Envy, Excessive Use of Literals, Too Many Parameters, Inconsistent Names, Conditional Complexity, Combinatorial Explosion, Oddball Solution, Lack of Standards and Conventions.

See Also

Abstraction, Divide-and-Conquer, Documentation Principle, Don't Repeat Yourself, Encapsulation, Information Hiding, Maximize Cohesion, Minimize Coupling, Modularity, Non-Redundancy Principle, Separation of Concerns

High Cohesion (HIC)

Also Known As: Maximize Cohesion

Original Contributors: W. Stevens, G. Myers, Larry Constantine, Meilir Page-Jones, and Ed Yourdon

> Maximize cohesion where possible.

Cohesion is a measure of how strongly-related or focused the responsibilities of a single module are. It measures the single-minded of a class, object or method in a system.

Larry Constantine first identified cohesion as a design principle in 1975 as part of his structured design process. He enumerated seven types of cohesion:

1. Coincidental cohesion happens when the parts of module have nothing in common (Example: Utility classes)
2. Logical cohesion happens when there is some logical relationship between elements of a module (Example: Data access methods for an Entity)
3. Temporal cohesion happens when elements grouped together are involved in activities that are related in time (Example: Set of functions responsible for initialization, start-up, the shutdown of a process)
4. Procedural cohesion happens when elements are grouped together because they always follow a certain sequence of execution (Example: a

method which checks file permissions and then opens the file)

5. Communicational (or Informational) Cohesion happens when all functions of a module refer to or update the same data structure (Example: Finder/Query methods on Entity using its key identifier)

6. Sequential cohesion happens when parts of a module are grouped because the output from one part is the input to another part like an assembly line (e.g. a method which reads data from a database table and processes the data)

7. Functional cohesion happens when parts of a module are grouped because they all contribute to a single well-defined task of the module (Example: A stack abstraction with methods to push, pop and check whether it is empty)

The below diagram represents the strengths of various cohesion types on a spectrum:

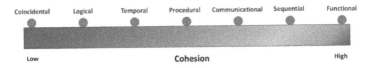

Peter Coad and Ed Yourdon classified cohesion in object-oriented systems into three categories:

- Method Cohesion – A method should do only one thing. A method that performs more than one task is very difficult to understand.
- Class Cohesion – is about the level of cohesion between the attributes and methods of a class. A

class should represent only one thing. All attributes of the class must be required to represent the thing.

- Generalization/Specialization Cohesion – is about how classes in a hierarchy are related.

Low cohesion leads to many issues like:

- High complexity – difficult to understand what belongs to where and why
- Poor reuse
- Poor readability

A heuristic to maximise cohesion: Try to summarize the purpose of a single module in a single phrase. If it turns out to be difficult to capture the purpose of a module into a single phrase, then that's an indicator of low cohesion.

Symptoms that indicate low cohesion:

- A class looks like a random set of functions
- Methods that don't interact with rest of the class
- Fields that are used by only one method
- Classes that change together (an indication that they need to be refactored into a separate class with high cohesion)

Also remember that maximising cohesion should not lead to adverse effect on minimizing coupling. i.e.: Don't go overboard by making everything a separate module to maximise cohesion; it will increase the number of dependencies between modules, and hence leading to strong coupling.

Quality Attributes Affected

Improves: Flexibility, Reusability, Testability, Maintainability, Readability

Reduces: Complexity

Metrics

Lack of Cohesion of Methods (LCOM), Information flow based Cohesion, Tight Class Cohesion, Loose Class Cohesion

Smells

Big Ball of Mud, Divergent Change, God Class, Large Class, Mixed Abstractions, Swiss Army Knife

See Also

Common Closure Principle, Common Reuse Principle, Maximize Cohesion, Pure Fabrication, Release Reuse Equivalence Principle, Single Responsibility Principle, Tell Don't Ask

Loose Coupling (LCO)

Also Known As: Minimize Coupling

Original Contributors: W. Stevens, G. Myers, Larry Constantine, Meilir Page-Jones, and Ed Yourdon

> Minimize coupling between components.
> or
> Strive for loosely coupled design between objects that interact.

Coupling is the degree of interdependence between two components. It measures how closely connected two components or modules are. Coupling indicates the degree of direct knowledge that one component has about another. Larry Constantine first identified coupling as a design principle and described several types of coupling, which are listed below:

- Content coupling (also known as Pathological Coupling) happens when a component accesses or modifies the local data of another component
- Common coupling happens when components/modules are bound together by global data structures
- External coupling happens when components rely on common external protocol or format
- Control coupling happens when a component decides the function of another and changes the flow of its execution

- Stamp coupling happens when multiple components share a common data structure and only parts of it
- Data coupling happens when components share data through parameters
- Message coupling happens when a component calls a method but does not pass any parameters

The following continuum depicts various coupling types with an indication on how tight (avoid) or lose (preferred) each type is.

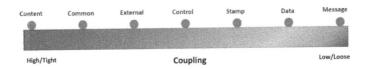

Minimizing coupling makes a component or module as independent as possible. Low coupling between modules indicates a well-partitioned system. Coupling can be reduced through:

- Eliminating unnecessary relationships
- Reducing the number of necessary relationships and
- Easing the "tightness" of the necessary relationships

Loose coupling reduces the risk that a change made within one element will create unanticipated changes within other components. Minimizing interconnections can help isolate problems when things go wrong and simplify testing, maintenance and troubleshooting procedures.

Quality Attributes Affected

Improves: Flexibility, Reusability, Testability, and Maintainability

Reduces: Complexity, Coupling

Metrics

Afferent Coupling (Ca), Efferent Coupling (Ce), Coupling Between Objects (CBO), Data Abstraction Coupling (DAC), Message Passing Coupling (MPC), and Coupling Factor (CF).

Smells

Cyclic Dependency, Solution Sprawl, Temporal Coupling, Dense Object Network, Hard Coded Dependencies, Hardcoded Resources, Method Chains, Inappropriate Intimacy, Violated Layering, Large Class, Large Package, Unnecessary Dependencies, Swiss Army Knife

See Also

Acyclic Dependencies Principle, Creator, Dependency Inversion Principle, Encapsulation, Information Hiding, Interface Segregation Principle, Inversion of Control, Law of Demeter, Program to an Interface, Separation of Interface and Implementation, Stable Abstraction Principle, Stable Dependencies Principle

Core Principles

This section describes a set of fundamental design principles that every developer should be familiar with.

Abstraction (ABS)

Also Known As: N/A

Original Contributors: Community Wisdom

> Model (reduce the characteristics of) real word entities into a set of objects with essential characteristics (state, behaviour and relationships) relevant to the context.

Abstraction is a process through which you narrow down to the relevant data and behaviour and ignore details not necessary for the context of the system under consideration. Abstraction helps to hide the complexity of the implementation and provides an interface which can be implemented later in any number of ways.

Abstraction is always specific to a context as the main goal is to isolate those aspects that are important for the purpose and suppress or ignore the ones that are unimportant. It is possible to have many different abstractions of the same thing, depending on the context for which they are made. For example: A Person becomes an Employee in the context of a Payroll Processing System, a Student in the context of a University Enrolment System and a Patient in the context of a Hospital Management System.

Abstraction is the most fundamental of all the programming principles. Data abstraction and procedural abstraction has been practiced from the beginning of programming. All programming languages

33

provide constructs to support both data and procedural abstractions. Advent of object-oriented programming lead to a new construct that combined data and behavioural abstractions into one entity called class.

Quality Attributes Affected

Improves: Cohesion

Reduces: Complexity, Coupling

Metrics

Coupling, Cohesion, Sufficiency, Completeness and Primitiveness

Smells

Primitive Obsession, Data Clump, Incomplete Abstraction, Unnecessary Abstraction, Unused Classes

See Also

Encapsulation, Inheritance, Don't Repeat Yourself

Information Hiding (IFH)

Also Known As: N/A

Original Contributors: David Parnas

> Hide design decisions which are subject to change within a module (function or procedure) and provide access to the module through well-defined interfaces that reveal only the required information to use the module.

Information Hiding is the most fundamental design principle that leads to self-contained modules which can change with little or no impact to other modules. Parnas introduced information hiding as a criterion for decomposing software system into modules. A design decision that is likely to change should be hidden in a module. There by keeping the changeable decision as a secret of the module. This approach promotes the goal of design for change.

Information hiding is applicable to all programming paradigms and implemented through subroutines or functions or procedures in programming languages. Object oriented paradigm extends the concept of information hiding through Encapsulation.

Quality Attributes Affected

Improves: Cohesion, Data Integrity, Modifiability, Modularity, Reliability

Reduces: Complexity, Coupling

Metrics

Number of Public Attributes, Demeter Distance

Smells

Deceptive Modularity, Too much Information Hiding, Excessive Encapsulation

See Also

Abstraction, Encapsulation, Separation of Concerns, Modularity

Encapsulation (ENC)

Also Known As: N/A

Original Contributors: Community Wisdom

> Group related ideas into a single unit and control (hide/protect) the visibility of attributes, methods, classes and modules from clients to avoid dependency on things that might change.

Encapsulation is all about compartmentalizing and hiding the internal mechanisms and data structures of a component behind a well-defined interface. Thus, enabling the users to know only what the component does and not depend on how it does it. Encapsulation helps to create self-contained units that can be easily modified or replaced without affecting any other parts of the system.

Encapsulation is a way to realize Information Hiding in object-oriented programming.

An attribute or a method of a class is encapsulated if it could not be accessed by an object's clients. A class can also be encapsulated with in a package or namespace.

Quality Attributes Affected

Improves: Cohesion, Data Integrity, Modifiability, Modularity, Reliability

Reduces: Complexity, Coupling

Metrics

Number of Public Attributes, Demeter Distance

Smells

Deficient Encapsulation, Excessive Encapsulation, Leaky Encapsulation, Missing Encapsulation, Trespassing Encapsulation, Unexploited Encapsulation, Open Doors

See Also

Abstraction, Information Hiding, Encapsulate What Varies, Separation of Concerns, Law of Demeter, Immutability

Inheritance (INH)

Also Known As: N/A

Original Contributors: Community Wisdom

Model Is-A relationship using inheritance.

Inheritance allows to use an existing type to derive a new type. Derived types inherit the attributes and methods of the super type. Derived types can override existing methods and add new attributes and methods. Inheritance allows us to support generalization through polymorphism as well as code reuse. Inheritance is most frequently misused as code reuse mechanism than a generalization mechanism. This principle provides clear guidance on when it is appropriate to use in inheritance as part of your design.

IS-A relationship denotes an "object is a type of another". Consider using inheritance to model IS-A relationship. In other words, inheritance may be appropriate design choice when polymorphic behaviour is required. Be judicious in using inheritance as it can lead to more complex designs and affect the testability. Composition is a better alternative to inheritance from a code reuse perspective.

Quality Attributes Affected

Improves: Reusability, Coupling (-ve)

Reduces: Duplication, Encapsulation (-ve), and Testability (-ve)

Metrics

Depth of Inheritance Tree(DIT), Number of Children (NOC), Total Children Count(TCC), Total Progeny Count (TPC), Total Parent Count (TPAC), Total Ascendancy Count (TAC), Total length of inheritance chain (TLI), Average Inheritance Depth (AID), Number of Methods Inherited (NMI), Number of Methods Overridden (NMO), Number of New Methods (NNA), Number of Ancestor Classes (NAC), Number of Descendent Classes (NDC), Class Complexity due to Inheritance (CCI), Average Complexity of a program due to Inheritance (ACI)

Smells

Cyclic Hierarchy, Parallel Inheritance Hierarchies, Missing Hierarchy, Unnecessary hierarchy, Wide Hierarchy, Unfactored Hierarchy, Speculative Hierarchy, Deep Hierarchy, Multipath Hierarchy, Rebellious Hierarchy, Broken Hierarchy

See Also

Abstraction, Encapsulation, Favour Composition Over Inheritance, Liscov Substitution Principle, Principle of Closed Behaviour

Polymorphism (POL)

Also Known As: N/A

Original Contributors: Community Wisdom

Use polymorphism when you need to provide single interface for accessing multiple related behaviours.

Polymorphism allows you to create multiple methods that have the same name but provide different implementations. The main advantage of polymorphism is that it simplifies the programming interface through reusing method names. There are two types of polymorphism:

1. Compile-time polymorphism or static polymorphism
   - Method Overloading is the most common form static polymorphism
   - Overloading supports methods with same name but different signatures and implementations
   - In this case, the compiler knows the object type it needs to link to and the specific method to call during compile time so it's called early binding
2. Run-Time polymorphism or Dynamic polymorphism
   - Method Overriding is used to implement this type of polymorphism
   - Overriding methods have the same name and signature but different implementations

in a parent and derived types of an inheritance tree
- In this case, the compiler would not know the specific method implementation to be called at compile time and it can be determined only during run-time and referred to as late binding

Dynamic languages like Ruby support a form of polymorphism referred to as Duck Typing.

Quality Attributes Affected

Improves: Reusability, Extensibility, Maintainability

Reduces: Duplication, Testability

Metrics

Number of Methods Overridden by a subclass (NMO) and Polymorphism Factor

Smells

Hiding Methods, Inadvertent Overload, Type Checking to Alter Behaviour, Casting

See Also

Abstraction, Encapsulation, Inheritance, Liscov Substitution Principle, and Principle of Closed Behaviour

Don't Repeat Yourself (DRY)

Also Known As: Avoid Duplication, Once and Only Once, Duplication is Evil (DIE) Principle

Original Contributors: Andrew Hunt and Dave Thomas

> Every piece of knowledge must have a single, unambiguous, authoritative representation within a system.

Duplication is the most common cause for poor maintainability. Duplication can be classified into two types: mechanical and knowledge.

Mechanical Duplication: Copy & Paste code is the most common form of mechanical duplication and may help to getting things up and running quickly but it makes code fragile and hard to change.

Knowledge Duplication: Reintroducing existing functionality through writing new code (usually not immediately recognized as duplication) with different name, abstractions and may be better implementation.

Mechanical duplication is easy to identify as well as fix whereas knowledge duplication is difficult both to identify and fix.

Duplication can happen in code (both production and test code), configuration, data model, documentation and any other artefact that is used as part of developing and maintaining a system.

Recognizing and eliminating duplication through proper abstraction and other best practices will produce a system that is flexible and maintainable.

Quality Attributes Affected

Improves: Reusability, Testability, and Maintainability

Reduces: Complexity

Metrics

Code Duplication

Smells

Copy Paste Reuse, Duplicated Code, Data Redundancy, Derived Value, Repeated Value, Alternative Modules with Different Interfaces, Magic Number

See Also

Abstraction, Encapsulation, Information Hiding, Inheritance, Manage Complexity, Minimize Coupling

Program to an Interface (P2I)

Also Known As: N/A

Original Contributors: Erich Gamma, Richard Helm, Ralph Johnson, and John Vlissides

> Program to an interface, not an implementation.

Program to an interface is about managing dependencies. It is the first principle mentioned in the GoF book and forms the basis for many of the patterns describe in it.

It is easy to add a dependency to a concrete implementation but getting rid of an unwanted dependency could potentially lead to refactoring and hinder reuse of code in another context. According to this principle, it is more beneficial to depend on an interface than a concrete implementation. When you depend only on interfaces, you are automatically decoupled from the implementation. The major advantage of adhering to this principle is that it allows clients to be decoupled from the implementation and you can add new behaviour without breaking clients.

Rule of thumb for adherence: Whenever possible use interfaces as part of method signatures (both parameters and return types) and variable declarations.

Quality Attributes Affected

Improves: Flexibility, Reusability and Maintainability

Reduces: Coupling

Metrics

Coupling

Smells

Hard Binding (References to specific implementation types instead of interface types)

See Also

Abstraction, Dependency Inversion Principle, Encapsulation, Inheritance, Inversion of Control, Separation of Interface and Implementation

Composite Reuse Principle (CRP)

Also Known As: Favour Composition over Inheritance

Original Contributors: Erich Gamma, Richard Helm, Ralph Johnson, and John Vlissides

Favour object composition over class inheritance.

Inheritance and Composition are two mechanisms supported by object-oriented programming to extend the functionality of existing code and reuse. Each of these mechanisms has its own advantages and disadvantages.

Here are some of the disadvantages of inheritance:

- Difficult to change the behaviour at runtime
- Hard to gain knowledge about all behaviours of the subtypes
- Leads to class explosion
- Difficult to write unit tests
- Changes to the base type can unintentionally affect some of the subtypes

Composition is an alternative to inheritance. Composition can be used to overcome all of these disadvantages. Composition allows for dynamically switching an implementation by delegating calls to appropriate objects at runtime. It's also referred to as dynamic/simulated inheritance. Favouring composition over inheritance will reduce maintainability problems as well as provide the flexibility to change the behaviour at run-time.

It is important to note that Composition and Inheritance are complementary and can be used together to achieve better designs.

Strategy pattern is a classic example which uses composition and delegation to change the context's behaviour without touching the context. The increased flexibility comes from the fact that you can plug-in different strategy objects and, that you can even change the strategy objects dynamically at run-time.

Quality Attributes Affected

Improves: Reusability, Testability, Maintainability, Flexibility, Extensibility

Reduces: Code Bloating, Coupling

Metrics

Depth of Inheritance Tree and Number of Child Classes

Smells

Combinatorial Explosion, Deep Class Inheritance Hierarchy

See Also

Abstraction, Encapsulation, Inheritance, Polymorphism, Program to an Interface, Open Closed Principle

Encapsulate What Varies (EWV)

Also Known As: N/A

Original Contributors: Erich Gamma, Richard Helm, Ralph Johnson, and John Vlissides

> Encapsulate the concept that varies.

Changes in requirements usually lead to redesign. It is impossible to predict the specifics of future requirements but easier to determine what aspects are likely to change. So instead of focusing on the cause for redesign, consider what you want to be able to change without redesign.

Most of the design patterns use encapsulation and composition to hide the potential variation behind an interface which makes it easier implement changes without redesign. During software design look for the aspects most likely to change and make provisions support them to protect the rest of the system from that change. This is called encapsulating variation.

Quality Attributes Affected

Improves: Extensibility, Maintainability

Metrics

N/A

Smells

Combinatorial Explosion, Divergent Change, Shotgun Surgery

See Also

Abstraction, Inheritance, Open Closed Principle

Modularity Principle (MOD)

Also Known As: Modularization Principle

Original Contributors: Gauthier Richard, Pont Stephen, Dijkstra, E. W, David L. Parnas, Bertrand Meyer

> Decompose a large system into a number of small manageable modules.

The concept of module is based on the idea of information hiding. Modules are well defined black boxes which can be replaced easily.

The Dictionary of the Object Technology defines modularity as: "The logical and physical decomposition of things (e.g., responsibilities and software) into small, simple groupings (e.g., requirements and classes, respectively), which increase the achievements of software-engineering goals."

The fundamental idea behind modularity is to organize the system as a set of modules with clear boundaries which can be developed independently and then plugged together. The idea may appear simple but the effectiveness depends on how the system is decomposed and the approach used to plug modules together to form the complete system. Modularity refers to reusability and extendibility together.

Modularity helps to achieve the following objectives:

- Manage complexity and improve comprehensibility
- Enable parallel work; and
- Accommodate future change

While most of the design principles focus on logical design, modularity focuses on both logical and physical design aspects. Language constructs such as Classes and Packages can be considered as modules as part of logical design. Physical design issues like determining which classes belong in which deployable units and managing the relationships between deployable units also need to be addressed to ensure the dependencies between the physical entities are optimal to realise the benefits modularity promises.

Kirk Knoernschild in his book Java Application Architecture define module as, "A software module is a deployable, manageable, natively reusable, composable, stateless unit of software that provides a concise interface to consumers." This definition succinctly summarizes the key characteristics of a module. A JAR/Assembly would qualify as a module in the Java/.NET platform.

Quality Attributes Affected

Improves: Modularity, Cohesion, Reusability, Testability, Maintainability

Reduces: Complexity, Coupling

Metrics

Fan-in, Fan-out, System Cyclicality, Intercomponent Cyclicality, Instability, Abstractness, Coupling, Cohesion, Sharability, Locality of Change

Smells

Big Ball of Mud, Circular dependencies between Packages, Circular dependencies between jars, subtype knowledge, Abstraction without decoupling, Degenerated inheritance, Deceptive Modularity.

See Also

Maximize Cohesion, Minimize Coupling, Package Design Principles, Separation of Concerns, Single Responsibility Principle

Closed Layered Architecture Principle (CLA)

Also Known As: N/A

Original Contributors: Community Wisdom

> Prefer closed layered architecture over open layered architecture. Allow each layer to communicate only with the layer immediately below it.

It is a common practice to separate an application into a set of distinct layers with well-defined interfaces to abstract the implementation referred to as Layered Architecture. It can be further classified into two types based on the restrictions imposed on the communication between layers:

1. Open Layered Architecture
2. Closed Layered Architecture

Open layered architecture allows a layer to communicate with any other layer above or below it and does not place any restrictions as depicted below. It leads to increased dependency and allows cyclic dependencies. The below diagram is an example for open layered architecture.

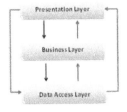

Closed layered architecture allows a layer to communicate only with the layer immediately below it. It minimizes the dependencies between layers so it is preferable over the open layered model. The below diagram is an example for a closed layered architecture.

Quality Attributes Affected

Improves: Cohesion, Modularity, and Maintainability

Reduces: Coupling

Metrics

Number of class/package cycles

Smells

Cyclic Dependency, Violated Layering

See Also

Dependency Inversion Principle, Minimize Coupling, Modularity, Separation of Concerns

Separation of Concerns (SoC)

Also Known As: N/A

Original Contributors: Edsger W. Dijkstra

Separate an application into units, with minimal overlapping between the functions of the individual units.

The fundamental idea behind separation of concerns is, decompose the system into parts with no or little overlap in functionality. It promotes the separation of various aspects of a problem, addressing them individually without requiring detailed knowledge of the other parts, and finally combining them into one result. SoC ensures changes to one part of the program do not impact other parts of the program by localising changes.

A concern is anything that is of interest to some stakeholder, whether an end user, a project sponsor, or even a developer. Concerns are reflections of system requirements and priorities of stakeholders in the system. Concerns can be classified into the following categories:

- Core concern: Generally, a functional requirement - a specific functionality to be included in a system. E.g.: Ability to allow a customer to deposit or withdraw from his savings account in a banking system.
- Crosscutting concern: Also referred to as an aspect is a non-functional behaviour of the system. A

concern that cuts across multiple modules. In general, they apply to the system as whole rather than to individual requirements. E.g.: Security, Logging, Caching.

The idea of SoC is so central that it appears in many different forms in the evolution of software design methodologies and programming languages. SoC is most commonly achieved using modularization, layering, encapsulation and Aspect Oriented Programming techniques. Pattern Example: MVC.

Quality Attributes Affected

Improves: Modularity, Testability, Cohesion, Reusability, and Maintainability

Reduces: Complexity, Coupling

Metrics

Coupling Between Concerns, Component-level Interlacing Between Concerns (CIBC), Interface-level Interlacing Between Concerns (IIBC), Operation-level Overlapping Between Concerns (OOBC), Afferent Coupling Between Components (AC), Efferent Coupling Between Components (EC), Lack of Concern-based Cohesion(LCC)

Smells

Scattering and Tangling

See Also

Modularity, Abstraction, Encapsulation, Single Responsibility Principle, Don't Repeat Yourself

Separate Policy and Implementation (SPI)

Also Known As: Separate Mechanism from Policy

Original Contributors: Per Brinch Hansen

> A component of a software system should deal with policy or implementation, but not both.

Let us first understand what a policy component and an implementation component is.

- A policy component makes a context sensitive decision which could vary based on a number of parameters. It is mostly application specific and subject to change.
- An implementation component deals with how to accomplish a task and does not depend on the context. The context independence makes it to be easier to reuse and maintain.

For example, allowing the user to choose the column and type of sorting in a spreadsheet is a good candidate to be a policy with separate components for implementing the sorting algorithms.

Separating the policy and Implementation allows for greater flexibility without changing the implementation. If it is not possible to separate policy and implementation into different components, there should at least be a clear separation of policy and implementation functionality within a component. The Strategy pattern is a good example that applies this principle.

Quality Attributes Affected

Improves: Flexibility and Reusability

Reduces: Complexity, and Coupling

Metrics

N/A

Smells

Conditional statements for selecting desired behaviour.

See Also

Minimize Coupling, Separation of Concerns, Program to an Interface, Separate Interface and Implementation, Inheritance, Favour Composition Over Inheritance

Separate Interface and Implementation (SII)

Also Known As: Interface Oriented Design

Original Contributors: Erich Gamma, Richard Helm, Ralph Johnson, and John Vlissides

> An abstraction should be decoupled from its implementation.

This principle is the core idea behind interface-oriented programming. Interface oriented programming is a discipline of programming that is based on the separation of public interface of the component from its implementation. Any component should consist of two parts:

1. A public interface that defines all the functionality provided by the component and accessible to a client.
2. An implementation which includes the actual code for the functionality provided by the component. The implementation can include additional functions and data structures that are only used internally within the component. The implementation is not directly accessed by the clients. It's widespread practice to specify which implementation to use through configuration and allow it to be injected at runtime.

61

This practice helps to protect a component's clients from its implementation details. Further, this principle allows you to implement the functionality of a component independently of its use by other components. A component can easily change when its interface is separated from its implementation. This separation prevents clients from being directly affected by any such changes. Bridge pattern is a good example where the separation of interface and implementation is addressed.

Quality Attributes Affected

Improves: Reusability, and Maintainability

Reduces: Coupling

Metrics

Number of interfaces implemented by a component

Smells

Hard Binding (Compile-time binding of the implementation)

See Also

Abstraction, Encapsulation, Inheritance, Program to an Interface, Hollywood Principle

Divide-and-Conquer (DAC)

Also Known As: N/A

Original Contributors: Community Wisdom

> Partition a complex system into multiple components, and then deal with these individual components to reduce complexity.

Dealing with something large all at once is much harder than dealing with a series of smaller things is the central premise of this principle. It is well known from the design of combinatorial algorithm designs like Quick Sort and Merge Sort. This principle is very useful in software design as well and provides many advantages. It divides a task or component into smaller parts that can be designed and developed independently. This allows an individual developer to specialize on individual aspects and makes it easier to understand. Parts can be replaced or changed without having to replace or extensively change other parts. Divide-and-Conquer also provides a way to realize the principle of modularity and separation of concerns.

Quality Attributes Affected

Improves: Modularity, Testability and Maintainability

Reduces: Complexity

Metrics

Number of Large Methods, Number of Large Classes
and Number of Large Packages

Smells

Large Method, Large Class, Large Package

See Also

Modularity, Separation of Concerns, Minimize
Complexity

Inversion of Control (IOC)

Also Known As: Hollywood Principle, Dependency Injection

Original Contributors: Erich Gamma, Richard Helm, Ralph Johnson, and John Vlissides

Don't call us, we'll call you.

"Don't call us, we will call you" is a typical response you would hear after auditioning for a role in a Hollywood movie. Understanding how this principle applies to software development is critical for developing large complex systems that use frameworks. It's a major paradigm shift for beginners. When you write a simple program, the control starts with the first statement in the main method and keeps flowing down as it instructed by the developer until the last statement gets executed. In other words, the programmer controls the flow of execution. Real life application development is not so simple and building enterprise applications require us to use frameworks. When developing an application that must fit into the constraints of a framework, you implement interfaces and get it registered mostly through a configuration mechanism supported by the framework. The framework calls the methods at appropriate times. Frameworks usually publish the life cycle of components and the interfaces to be implemented allowing control over structure and managing dependencies.

Events or call-backs using Observer pattern is a good example that implements this principle. It allows one to observe the state of an object and act (as and when required) in a well-defined and unobtrusive manner.

Dependency Injection (DI) is a form of Inversion of Control (IoC). DI is another well-known example for the use of the Hollywood principle. DI frameworks like Spring, Google Guice, Spring.Net and Unity are good examples which rely on this principle.

Quality Attributes Affected

Improves: Flexibility, Reuse, Testability, Maintainability

Reduces: Coupling

Metrics

Coupling Between Objects (CBO), Response For Class (RFC), Efferent Coupling (Ce), Afferent Coupling (Ca), Coupling Factor (CF), Number of Cyclic Dependencies

Smells

Too Many Dependencies, Cyclic Dependencies, Constructor Over Injection, Hard Binding.

See Also

Dependency Inversion Principle, Minimize Coupling, Program to an Interface, Separate Interface and Implementation

Plug and Play (PnP)

Also Known As: Plugin

Original Contributors: Community Wisdom

> Prefer plug and play mechanism for dynamic discovery of components to support extension and variation of implementation based on runtime.

The plug and play concept was originally introduced by the hardware and operating system developers to recognize and adapt to hardware configuration changes with little or no intervention by a user. Extending the application to software development, when building a product, we need a flexible, customizable design where features can be varied based on a customer requirement. To support the flexibility required, we should be able to:

- Use different implementations on multiple runtime environments
- Link components using configuration rather than compilation

Plug and play design provides this kind of flexibility. Proper application of Dependency Injection leads to loosely coupled code which makes it easier to "plug-and-play".

Patterns like Adapter, Bridge, Plugin are good examples which follow this principle.

Quality Attributes Affected

Improves: Extendibility, Testability

Reduces: Coupling

Metrics

N/A

Smells

Hard Binding, Scattered Configuration

See Also

Inversion of Control, Separate Interface and Implementation, Program to an Interface

Modular Protection (MOP)

Also Known As: N/A

Original Contributors: Bertrand Meyer

> Confine the effects of an abnormal condition occurring at run time in a module to that module, or at worst propagate to a few neighbouring modules.

Protection is one of the criteria used for evaluating modularity. It provides clear guideline on the propagation of runtime errors - avoid propagation of error conditions to neighbouring modules.

Examples:

- Validating input at the source. Every module that accepts data is responsible for checking the validity (before passing it to others) is good for modularity.
- A data control that supports an Error event, so that if an error occurs when the control is attempting to access the database, it can be dealt with within the control, and not propagate to other parts of the program.

Languages like Java and C# which support the notion of exception. In these languages, it is possible that an exception is "raised" by a certain instruction in one method/component and "handled" in another, possibly remote part of the system which is an undisciplined exception handling practice. Such language features make it possible to decouple algorithm for normal case processing and exceptional cases. But they must be used judiciously to avoid hindering modular protection. Undisciplined exceptions are a violation of this principle.

Quality Attributes Affected

Improves: Modularity and Maintainability

Reduces:

Metrics

Number of exceptions propagated

Smells

Throwing multiple exceptions

See Also

Disciplined Exception Handling, Modularity, Separation of Concerns

Discrimination Principle (DP)

Also Known As: N/A

Original Contributors: Bertrand Meyer

> Use unique values to describe a fixed number of possible cases. For classification of data abstractions with varying features, use inheritance.

Use unique values to describe a fixed number of possible cases. For classification of data abstractions with varying features, use inheritance.

The key idea behind this principle is conditionals (if/else) and multi-branch (switch/case) instructions should not be used as a substitute for implicit discrimination techniques of object-oriented design, based on dynamic binding.

If your implementation has type code or type branch smells, it is an indication that oriented design techniques are not applied properly. The design is more procedural and relies on conditionals to change the behaviour of methods. Using inheritance and polymorphism would lead to a more elegant solution.

Type Code smell occurs when a code (usually a set of numbers or strings form a list of allowable values) is used for representing a type of entity instead of a separate class.

Type Branch smell occurs when a conditional is used to change the behaviour.

The following refactorings can be applied to implement this principle depending on the context:

- Replace Type Code with Class
- Replace Type Code with Subclasses
- Replace Type Code with State/Strategy

Quality Attributes Affected

Improves: Reusability, Testability and Maintainability

Reduces: Complexity

Metrics

N/A

Smells

Type Code, Type Branch

See Also

Abstraction, Encapsulation, Inheritance, Polymorphism, Encapsulate What Varies

SOLID Principles

Robert C. Martin had collated five principles that lead to good design in the mid-1990s. Michael Feathers coined the acronym SOLID in the early 2000s as a mnemonic for remembering the principles.

SOLID is an acronym for five design principles:

- **S**ingle Responsibility Principle
- **O**pen Closed Principle
- **L**iskov Substitution Principle
- **I**nterface Segregation Principle
- **D**ependency Inversion Principle

This section covers these principles.

Single Responsibility Principle (SRP)

Also Known As: Class Consistency Principle (CCP)

Original Contributors: Bertrand Meyer, Robert C. Martin

> All the features of a class must pertain to a single, well-identified abstraction.[#]
> or
> A class should have only one reason to change.[##]

The single responsibility principle encourages us to design a class in such a way that there is only one reason for it to change. When a class has more than one reason to change, it has multiple responsibilities. A class with multiple responsibilities should be refactored to smaller classes, each with only one reason (responsibility) to change.

SRP can be traced back to Class Consistency principle described in Bertrand Meyer's Object-Oriented Software Construction which is based the idea of Connascence. Connascence introduced by Meiler Page Jones, generalises the notion of cohesion and coupling, and combines it with encapsulation. The central theme remains the same – maximize cohesion and minimize coupling.

Class cohesion is a measure of how single-minded a class is. Ideally a class should represent only one thing. All attributes and methods contained in a class must be required for the class to represent the thing. Moreover, there should not be any attributes or methods that are not used. In other words, a class should only have the attributes and methods that are necessary to fully define instances for the domain problem they represent.

A class with multiple responsibilities requires a large number of test cases to validate as the possibility of those responsibilities interacting in unintended ways. Having single responsibility makes testing easier.

Single responsibility usually leads to smaller classes and hence improving the readability and maintainability of the system.

Quality Attributes Affected

Improves: Cohesion, Testability and Maintainability

Reduces: Coupling

Metrics

Connascence, Cohesion, Coupling

Smells

Constructor Over-Injection, Divergent Change, High Coupling, Lack of Cohesion, Mixed Abstractions, Large Class, God Class, Swiss Army Knife, Big Ball of Mud.

See Also

Maximize Cohesion, Minimize Coupling, Law of Demeter, Separation of Concerns, Modularity

Class consistency principle coined by Bertrand Meyer. ## Single Responsibility Principles as described by Robert C. Martin

Open Closed Principle (OCP)

Also Known As: Protected Variations

Original Contributors: Bertrand Meyer, Alistair Cockburn

> Software entities (classes, modules, functions) should be open for extension, but closed for modification.

A unit of software is considered "open" for extension when it is easy to change the behaviour without modifying its code, i.e. "closed" for modification.

Here are some of the most common indicators that your code violates this principle:

- Using conditional code with if/else or switch/case to determine the strategy
- Hard coded references to other class names, type checking and casting
- Using new operator to create class objects

OCP promotes proper use of inheritance and polymorphism in design to drive extensibility with no or minimal side effects when extending. Proper abstraction using interfaces and base classes is key to apply OCP. You need to be judicious in applying this principle to come up with class hierarchies as inheritance and polymorphism themselves are complex in nature. Apply it only to the parts of the system that is more likely to change.

Strategy, Template Method and Abstract Factory are good examples for patterns that implement OCP.

Quality Attributes Affected

Improves: Extensibility, Modularity, Maintainability

Reduces: Coupling

Metrics

N/A

Smells

Conditional Code, Speculative Variation

See Also

Abstraction, Encapsulation, Information Hiding, Inheritance, Favour Composition Over Inheritance, Separate Interface and Implementation

Liscov Substitution Principle (LSP)

Also Known As: Principle of type conformance (or substitutability)

Original Contributors: Barbara Liscov

Subtypes must be substitutable for their base types.

A Type hierarchy is used to define type families consisting of a base type and its subtypes. Subtypes usually provide different implementations of their base type and can extend the behaviour of their base type, by providing additional methods. The substitution principle provides abstraction by specification for type families by mandating that subtypes behave in accordance with the specification of their base type. This allows using code to be written in terms of the base type specification, still work correctly when using objects of the subtype.

LSP is all about implementing behavioural subtyping (polymorphism) without altering any of the desirable properties of that program like correctness, task performed, etc. To be compliant with LSP, any derived type must be substitutable for base types. This guarantees that a client can consume any of the subtypes without worrying about the correctness of the system.

Subtypes must follow the below rules to comply with this principle:

- The subtype has all the attributes of base type

- The class invariant of the subtype is equal to or stronger than that of the base type
- For each of the operation that is overridden and redefined by subtype
  - Name of the operation must be the same as base type
  - The signature must correspond to base type operation's signature
  - Precondition must be equal to or weaker than base type operation. Input parameter type should be the same or its base type (i.e. input parameter can be widened/upcasted – contravariant argument is allowed)
  - Postcondition must be equal to or stronger than base type operation. Return type can be the same or its subtype (i.e. return type can be narrowed/downcasted – covariant return type is allowed)
  - Exceptions can be narrowed but no new exceptions can be thrown
- History constraint – subtype should not allow state changes that are not permissible in the base type

It is interesting to note that adherence to LSP is key for OCP conformance.

Quality Attributes Affected

Improves: Reusability, Reliability and Maintainability

Metrics

Depth of Inheritance, Width of Inheritance, Number of Methods Overridden

Smells

Broken Hierarchy, Type Checking, Conditional code to modify behaviour, Heavy Use of Reflection, Throws NotImplementedException

See Also

Abstraction, Inheritance, Polymorphism, Favour Composition Over Inheritance, Principle of Closed Behaviour, Minimize Complexity

Interface Segregation Principle (ISP)

Also Known As: N/A

Original Contributors: Robert C. Martin

Client should not be forced to depend upon methods that they do not use. Interfaces belong to clients, not to hierarchies.

Interface bloat happens when an interface has too many operations but most of the clients can't perform or require all the operations. It is also known as fat interface. Fat interfaces are not cohesive and include unnecessary dependencies that clients do not require. This principle provides the guidelines to deal with the disadvantages of fat interfaces.

Interfaces with a small number of methods are referred to as "Fine-grained Interfaces". Make fine-grained interfaces that are client specific, so it is meaningful from the client point of view. The dependency between one class to another should be on the smallest possible interface. Hence many client specific interfaces are better than one general purpose interface.

Quality Attributes Affected

Improves: Cohesion, Reusability, Testability and Maintainability

Reduces: Complexity and Coupling

Metrics

Lack of Cohesion of Methods, Number of Methods in an Interface

Smells

Fat Interface

See Also

Abstraction, Single Responsibility Principle, Minimize Coupling, Maximize Cohesion

Dependency Inversion Principle (DIP)

Also Known As: N/A

Original Contributors: Robert C. Martin

> High-level modules should not depend on low-level modules. Both should depend on abstractions. Abstractions should not depend upon details. Details should depend upon abstractions.

The key theme is inverting the dependency management. An object should not control creating its own dependencies. It should allow the caller to provide the dependencies through a dependency injection mechanism like Constructor Injection or Setter Injection. Using an Inversion of control framework like Spring makes it easy to implement this principle.

To adhere to this principle all you have to do is:

- Separate Interface and Implementation,
- Program to an interface and
- Use dependency injection pattern to manage an object's dependencies

Quality Attributes Affected

Improves: Reusability, Testability and Maintainability

Reduces: Coupling

Metrics

Abstractness

Smells

Hard Binding (hard coded dependencies), Use of new

See Also

Minimize Coupling, Inversion of Control, Program to an Interface, Separate Interface and Implementation, Creator

GRASP Principles

GRASP stands for General Responsibility Assignment Software Patterns (or Principles). Craig Larman coined this acronym and listed the following set of principles in his book, Applying UML and Patterns:

- Controller
- Creator
- High Cohesion
- Indirection
- Information Expert
- Low Coupling
- Polymorphism
- Protected Variations
- Pure Fabrication

Some of the principles: High Cohesion, Low Coupling, Polymorphism and Protected Variations are already covered in previous sections. I've not included Controller as it is a design pattern and Indirection or Delegation as its too primitive. This section covers rest of the GRASP principles.

Tell Don't Ask (TDA)

Also Known As: Expert Principle, Do it Myself Principle

Original Contributors: Alec Sharp, Craig Larman, Peter Coad

> Assign a responsibility to the information expert, that is, the class that has the information necessary to fulfil the responsibility.

Asking an object for data and acting on that data is an anti-pattern as it results in design that is more procedural than object-oriented, and it breaks encapsulation completely. The below diagram illustrates the Ask style design.

The ability to simply tell an object to do something, rather than getting the data and then doing different things based on it is a key feature of object-oriented programming. The below diagram illustrates the Tell style design.

The central idea behind this principle is responsibilities should be placed along with data. This principle is similar to real-life practice where an individual who has the necessary information is assigned the task that depends on those details. Following this principle leads to good object-oriented design which emphasises proper encapsulation, that is, combine data and process together. Properly applying this principle would lead to a collection of objects that expose behaviour often referred to as rich domain model. Do keep low coupling and high cohesion as key drivers to make the decision on assigning responsibilities so the design supports clear separation of concerns.

Quality Attributes Affected

Improves: Cohesion

Reduces: Coupling

Metrics

Demeter Distance, Coupling Between Objects

Smells

Anaemic Domain Model, God Object, Inappropriate Intimacy, Procedural Programming

See Also

Abstraction, Encapsulation, Maximize Cohesion, Minimize Coupling, Law of Demeter, Separation of Concerns

Creator (CRE)

Also Known As: N/A

Original Contributors: Craig Larman

A class B should be responsible for creating instances of class A if one, or preferably more, of the following apply:
- Instances of B contain or compositely aggregate instances of A
- Instances of B record instances of A
- Instances of B closely use instances of A
- Instances of B have the initializing information for instances of A and pass it on creation

Object creation is the most common activity in any system we build. Hence it is beneficial to have a general principle for assigning creation responsibilities. This principle provides clear guidelines on the criterion to be used to determine which class should be responsible for creating a new instance of another class.

When the complexity of object creation is significant, for example, using a pooled instance for better performance or instance creation is conditional based on external property, it's better to consider delegating the creation responsibilities to a Factory class or other appropriate creational pattern.

If you are using a dependency injection framework as part of your implementation, most of the creation responsibilities lie with the DI framework.

Quality Attributes Affected

Increases: Maintainability

Reduces: Coupling

Metrics

Coupling

Smells

Temporal Coupling, Solution Sprawl, New operator

See Also

Encapsulation, Inversion of Control, Minimize Coupling

Pure Fabrication (PUF)

Also Known As: N/A

Original Contributors: Craig Larman

> Assign a highly cohesive set of responsibilities to an artificial or convenience class that does not represent a problem domain concept – something made up to support high cohesion, low coupling and reuse.

When Maximize Cohesion and Minimize Coupling or other similar objectives drive the design, but the choices offered by other principles like Expert (for example) are not appropriate, which object should have the responsibilities? It is preferable to have software classes to represent the concepts in the real-world problem domain as it lowers representational gap. But there are many situations where assigning responsibilities only to the domain object leads to issues like low cohesion, higher coupling or low reuse potential. In such situations, assign the highly cohesive responsibilities to an artificial class. Such a made-up class is a fabrication and it supports high cohesion, low coupling and the design of the fabrication is pure, or clean so it a pure fabrication.

Pure Fabrication is the best alternative when solution offered by the Expert Principle leads to poor design.

Almost all the design patterns like Adapter, Strategy, Command, etc. are good examples of Pure Fabrications.

Quality Attributes Affected

Improves: Cohesion, Reuse

Reduces: Coupling

Metrics

Cohesion, Coupling

Smells

Low Cohesion, High Coupling

See Also

Expert, Maximize Cohesion, Minimize Coupling

Reliability Principles

Reliability - the ability of a component to perform its functions as expected under stated conditions is a non-negotiable attribute. This section describes a set of principles focused on improving the reliability of design.

Precondition Principle (PRP)

Also Known As: N/A

Original Contributors: Bertrand Meyer

> A client calling a feature must make sure that the precondition holds before the call.

A precondition is a predicate that must always be true just prior to the execution of a method. Preconditions usually define any constraints on the object state which are necessary for successful execution of a method. A precondition constitutes the caller's part of the contract. The caller is expected to oblige and ensure that the precondition holds before calling the method.

When using a contract driven design approach, it is reasonable to expect that every method precondition would satisfy the following criteria:

- The precondition is part of the official documentation distributed to the clients.
- The need for the precondition can be justified in terms of the specification of the task to be done. i.e. Supplier of the method should not place assertions just for implementation convenience.
- A precondition should not use features that are not exposed (private or protected) to the callers.

Violation of a precondition is an indication that there could be a potential bug in the caller's code. Having preconditions make it easy to test and debug.

Quality Attributes Affected

Improves: Reliability, Testability and Maintainability

Reduces: Complexity

Metrics

Number of Unit Test Failures, Number of Preconditions

Smells

Untested Code, Buggy Client

See Also

Postcondition Principle, Class Invariant Principle, Non-Redundancy Principle

Postcondition Principle (POP)

Also Known As: N/A

Original Contributors: Bertrand Meyer

> A feature must make sure that, if its precondition held at the beginning of its execution, its postcondition will hold at the end.

A post condition is a predicate that must always be true just after the execution of a method. A post condition is part of the supplier's contract and it offers assurance to the callers that in cases where the method is called in state in which the precondition holds, the properties declared by the postcondition are guaranteed.

Violation of a postcondition is an indication that there could be a potentially bug in the supplier's code. Having postconditions make it easy to test and debug.

Quality Attributes Affected

Improves: Reliability, Testability and Maintainability

Reduces: Complexity

Metrics

Number of Unit Test Failures, Number of Postconditions

Smells

Untested Code, Buggy Supplier

See Also

Postcondition Principle, Class Invariant Principle, Non-Redundancy Principle

Class Invariant Principle (CIP)

Also Known As: N/A

Original Contributors: Bertrand Meyer

> A class invariant must hold as soon as an object is created, then before and after the execution of any of the class features available to clients.

A class invariant is an assertion describing the property which holds for all instances of a class. For example, the invariant of a Collection could be stated as follows:

(0 <= count and count <= capacity)

Class invariants are consistency constraints characterizing the semantics of a class. An invariant is a general clause which applies to the complete set of contracts defining a class including precondition and postcondition. Invariants allow us to identify certain states as valid or invalid. Invariants and postconditions help us to identify constraints placed on states or state transitions and create additional synchronization and encapsulation requirements. For example: An operation must be made atomic if it has invalid state transitions. If certain states are invalid, then the underlying state variables must be encapsulated properly to prevent a client from leaving the object in an invalid state.

Quality Attributes Affected

Improves: Reliability, Testability and Maintainability

Reduces: Complexity

Metrics

Number of Unit Test Failures, Number of Class Invariants

Smells

Illegal State Exception Handlers, Synchronization Block/Method

See Also

Precondition Principle, Postcondition Principle, Non-Redundancy Principle

Non-Redundancy Principle (NRP)

Also Known As: N/A

Original Contributors: Bertrand Meyer

> Under no circumstances shall the body of a routine ever test for the routine's precondition.

This principle is counter to what defensive programming advocates. This principle originates from the notion of Design by Contract™ proposed by Bertrand Meyer. In contract driven design, a method's precondition is well defined, and it is the responsibility of the client to fulfil it. Failure of precondition implies the client is at fault and the supplier does not need to guarantee postconditions.

Languages like Scala provide functions which work in tandem to support contract driven design constructs:

- **require** - Blames the caller of the method for violating the precondition
- **ensuring** – Guarantees post condition

Typically, a precondition failure would abort the call blaming the client. Meyer calls this "Zen and the art of software reliability: guaranteeing more by checking less."

Quality Attributes Affected

Improves: Reliability, Testability and Maintainability

Reduces: Complexity

Metrics

Number of Unit Test Failures, Number of Preconditions

Smells

Compensating or cleaning-up input data, Buggy Client

See Also

Precondition Principle, Postcondition Principle, Class Invariant Principle

Note: Design by Contract is a trade mark of Eiffel Software.

Command-Query Separation Principle (CQS)

Also Known As: Separate Queries from Commands (SQC)

Original Contributors: Bertrand Meyer

Asking a question should not change the answer.

The fundamental idea behind this principle is an object's methods should be divided into two categories:

- Query: A method that returns a result but does not change the observable state of the object or the system. A query does not produce any side effect.
- Command: A method that may change the state of the object or the system but does not return a result.

This classification allows us to clearly separate methods that change state (produce side effect) from those don't. The classification is based on the function's return type, void for commands and a type for queries. It works well in most cases but there are situations where you may prefer not to follow it for brevity. For example, in the java idiom for a collection, next method returns the next item in the collection as well as advances the iterator. It is possible to come up with a design that follows this style using separate methods current and advance, but the designers of Java chose to not to follow this principle favouring the idiom.

Quality Attributes Affected

Improves: Reliability, Testability, Maintainability

Reduces: Coupling

Metrics

Number of Side Effects

Smells

Side Effects

See Also

Leave No Side Effects

Principle of Closed Behaviour (PCB)

Also Known As: N/A

Original Contributors: Barbara Liscov, Meilir Page-Jones

> For a subtype S of type T, the principle where by the behaviour of S – including that derived from T – does not violate the class invariant of any class of type S.

The Substitution Principle plays a very important role in designing sound type hierarchies. Conformance to substitution principle leads to sounds type hierarchies only in read-only scenarios, i.e. only when query operations are executed. It's not enough when it comes to scenarios where commands, modifier operations are executed. We need this Principle of Close Behaviour to handle the scenarios where modifier operations are executed. This principle mandates that the behaviour inherited by a subtype from a base type should satisfy the class invariant of the subtype. Without conformance to this principle, the design of subtypes with modifier operations would lead to error-prone behaviour.

Let us consider a simple example to illustrate.

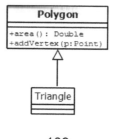

Scenario 1 - Polygon.area when applied on an object of Triangle preserves its "triangle-ness".

Scenario 2 – Polygon.addVertex when applied on an object of Triangle destroys the triangular property and it becomes a quadrilateral!

This illustrates the fact that closure of a subtype with respect to its base type's behaviour does not happen automatically and it needs to be designed explicitly by overriding the operations of the base type which would otherwise break the invariant of the subtype. In such a scenario, it is appropriate for the object to reject the message or simply take no action, not even throwing an exception. If this is not acceptable then it is most probably a case where inheritance is being force fitted. Check whether the IS-A relationship in this case really holds behaviourally and consider alternate design options.

Quality Attributes Affected

Improves: Reliability and Reuse

Metrics

Number of Subclass Invariants Violated

Smells

Broken Hierarchy

See Also

Inheritance, Polymorphism, Liscov Substitution Principle

Immutability (IMM)

Also Known As: N/A

Original Contributors: Community Wisdom

Favour immutability over mutability.

An object whose state cannot be modified after it is created is referred to as immutable. An object which can be modified after it is created is called mutable.

Mutability is not preferred as it leads to side effects and makes the code prone to race conditions leading to thread safety issues.

Here are some of the advantages of immutability:

- Simple to construct and use objects
- Thread-safety
- Helps to avoid temporal coupling
- Helps to avoid side effects
- Makes it easy to test

Immutability is a key tenet of functional programming as it is an enabling technique to write pure functions.

Quality Attributes Affected

Improves: Reliability, Testability

Reduces: Coupling (temporal)

Metrics

Number of Mutable Variables

Smells

Mutable Variables, Altered Parameter, Synchronized Method/Block

See Also

Law of Demeter, Leave No Side Effects

No Side Effects Principle (NSE)

Also Known As: Pure Functions

Original Contributors: Community Wisdom

> Strive for pure functions which leave no side effects.

A function produces side effect when it modifies some variable outside its scope or has observable interaction with outside world apart from returning a value. Here are some examples of side effects:

- Modifying a (global) variable
- Read from or write to a file
- Read user input from console
- Print to the console
- Throwing an exception

Side effects make it difficult to:

- Verify the correctness of a function
- Use functions to compose and create new behaviour
- Understand and debug

Side effects are the most common way a function interacts with the outside world. The degree to which side effects are used depends on the programming paradigm. Imperative programming is notorious for its frequent use of side effects. Functional programming avoids side effects. Some functional languages like Scala and Scheme don't restrict side effects but we can

113

avoid them. Stateful computation like I/O with side effects can be handled using monads.

Quality Attributes Affected

Improves: Reliability, Modularity, Testability and Maintainability

Reduces: Coupling

Metrics

Number of side effects

Smells

Side Effect, Temporal Coupling

See Also

Immutability, Command Query Separation, Design for Testability

Disciplined Exception Handling (DEH)

Also Known As: N/A

Original Contributors: Bertrand Meyer

> There are only two legitimate responses to an exception that occurs during the execution of a routine:
> 1. Retrying: attempt to change the conditions that led to the exception and to execute the routine again from the start.
> 2. Failure: clean up the environment, terminate the call and report failure to the caller.
>
> In addition, exceptions resulting from some cases may justify a false alarm response: determine that the exception is harmless and pick up the routine's execution where it started.

Most commonly used programming languages like Java and C# use exceptions as the primary method for error handling. This helps to separate error handling code from the normal processing logic and facilitate clear separation of concerns. This principle provides clear guidelines on how to respond to exceptions. To be more precise, simply ignoring an exception is not acceptable; a block must either be retried and successfully complete or propagate the exception to its caller. Care should be exercised to determine false alarms where it may be fine to ignore the exception and continue the execution.

Quality Attributes Affected

Improves: Reliability and Maintainability

Metrics

Number of Catch Blocks per Class (NCBC), Exception Handling Factor (EHF)

Smells

Empty Catch Blocks, Not closing resources in finally block

See Also

Modular Protection, Documentation Principle

Design for Testability (DFT)

Also Known As: Principle of Testability

Original Contributors: Wolfgang Pree

A class should be testable independently.

Classes are the building blocks of an object-oriented system. The degree to which a class facilitates testing using an automated unit testing framework is called testability. Dependencies and Observability of a class are the key factors that affect testability.

A class may have dependency on one or more classes. Dependencies are necessary for functionality but make testing difficult. Hardwired dependencies on classes and system resources, high coupling, cyclic dependencies, a dense network of object links are especially problematic for testing.

Ability to observe the return values, intermediate computation results, the sequence of method calls, and the occurrence of faults during and after execution of test is referred to as observability. Provide a standard-test interface to read and write object state to make a class observable and improve testability

During unit test we want to test a class in isolation which is the premise behind this principle, i.e. it should be possible to test the correctness of a class independently.

There a number of design techniques that can be employed to improve the testability of design, for example:

- Limit the use of class inheritance and polymorphism
- Avoid non-determinism
- Avoid too complex classes

Quality Attributes Affected

Improves: Testability, Reliability and Maintainability

Reduces: Coupling

Metrics

Code Coverage, Branch Coverage, Potentially Problematic Class Interactions, Coupling

Smells

Circular Dependencies, Hard Coded Dependencies, Hardcoded Resources, Dense Object Network, Information Loss, Non-Local Faults, Unobservable

See Also

Minimize Coupling, Maximize Cohesion, Minimize Complexity, Precondition Principle, Postcondition Principle, Class Invariant Principle

Package Design Principles

Packages help to organize classes in large systems to make them manageable. This section describes a set of six principles to determine package cohesion and package coupling.

Package Cohesion Principles

The following principles help to determine which classes should be grouped together into which packages:

- Reuse-release Equivalence Principle (REP)
- Common-Reuse Principle (CRP)
- Common-Closure Principle (CCP)

Package Coupling Principles

The following principles help to determine how the packages should relate to each other:

- Acyclic Dependencies Principle (ADP)
- Stable-Dependencies Principle (SDP)
- Stable-Abstractions Principle (SAP)

Release Reuse Equivalency Principle (REP)

Also Known As: N/A

Original Contributors: Robert C. Martin

> The granule of reuse is the granule of release. This granule is the package.

There are different forms of reuse. Copy paste code is the easiest form of reuse, but it would lead to maintenance nightmare as the responsibility to make changes, fix bugs and test them lies with the same team. It rarely makes sense to release individual classes for reuse. A more effective way to reuse is to group reusable components together in a package and release it with documentation. It is preferred to depend only on the documentation to reuse components rather than looking into source code to be able to use them.

It is a best practice to treat reusable software components as external software and maintain them separately, version control and release them as black-box packages. Class library distributed as a complete black-box package makes it effective for reuse. This allows users of the reusable package to choose when to integrate the changes from the package into their own code.

Quality Attributes Affected

Improves: Cohesion, Reusability, and Maintainability

Reduces: Coupling

Metrics

Package cohesion (PCoh)

Smells

Large Package, Cyclic Dependency, Unnecessary Dependency

See Also

Maximize Cohesion, Minimize Coupling, Common Closure Principle, Common Reuse Principle

Common Closure Principle (CCP)

Also Known As: N/A

Original Contributors: Robert C. Martin

> The classes in a package should be closed together against the same kind of changes. A change that affects a package affects all the classes in that package.

This is a variation of SRP as it applies to packages. SRP mandates that a class should have only one reason to change, similarly CCP mandates that a package (the unit of reusable classes or components) should not have multiple reasons to change. The key theme behind this principle is to limit changes to as few packages as possible. Being closed against the same kind of changes is referred to as common closure. In this context, it means when something needs to change, it is highly desired that the change requested affects only one package rather than distributed through multiple packages. Classes in a package should be closed to the same kinds of changes.

If two classes are tightly coupled either logically or physically, it is highly likely that they would change together. So, tightly coupled classes belong to the same package. This helps to confine changes, minimize workload related to revalidating and redistributing the package. This also minimizes the frequency of packages releases.

Quality Attributes Affected

Improves: Cohesion, Modularity and Maintainability

Reduces: Coupling

Metrics

Package cohesion (PCoh)

Smells

Large Package

See Also

Single Responsibility Principle, Modularity, Separation of Concerns, Maximize Cohesion, Minimize Coupling

Common Reuse Principle (CRP)

Also Known As: N/A

Original Contributors: Robert C. Martin

> The classes in a package are reused together. If you reuse one of the classes in a package, you reuse them all.

The REP emphasises the importance of using a package for releasing reusable components. It is essential to decide which classes should be packaged together. An improper selection of classes into a package can lead to unnecessary dependencies and make reuse difficult. This principle provides guidance on how to decide which classes are grouped together into a package.

Group reusable components into a package based on expected usage by clients, not on common functionality or any other arbitrary classification. Group classes that are reused based on collaborations between library classes. Classes that are used together are packaged together.

Remember the unit of reuse is the entire package even if just one or two classes are being used by a client. Keep classes that aren't reused together in separate packages. This minimize the dependencies, testing and revalidation efforts when there is a change for the clients who are reusing the packages.

Quality Attributes Affected

Improves: Cohesion, Reusability and Maintainability

Reduces: Coupling

Metrics

Package cohesion (PCoh)

Smells

Monolithic Package – Fat JAR, Unnecessary Dependencies

See Also

Common Closure Principle, Dependency Inversion, Open Closed Principle, Minimize Coupling, Maximize Cohesion

Acyclic Dependencies Principle (ADP)

Also Known As: N/A

Original Contributors: Robert C. Martin

Allow no cycles in the package dependency graph.

When two or more packages are involved in a dependency cycle, it becomes very difficult to stabilize the application. Changes to any package in the cycle result in changes being required in every other package in the cycle. It also becomes harder to isolate packages for testing purposes or to extract packages for reuse in a different context, because you end up transitively depending on every other package in the cycle. A naive automated build system can be completely defeated by a cycle in the package graph, getting stuck in an infinite loop of constant rebuilding.

Let us say there are three packages A, B and C with the following dependencies:

- Package A depends on B
- Package B depends on C
- Package C depends on A

We can visualize the dependencies using a directed graph where each of the vortex represents a package and the dependencies between them an edge as depicted below.

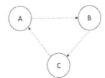

This above directed graph has a cycle (there is a path via different vertices that leads back to the original vertex). The dependency structure between packages must be a directed acyclic graph, that is, there must be no cycles in the dependency structure. The below graph is an example for a directed acyclic graph (no cycles).

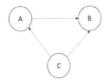

You can break cycles through any of the following mechanisms:

- Dependency Inversion Principle along with an IoC container
- Common Reuse Principle to split packages
- Reorganizing packages

Quality Attributes Affected

Improves: Reusability and Maintainability

Reduces: Coupling

Metrics

Number of Cyclic Dependencies

Smells

Cyclic Dependency

See Also

Minimize Coupling, Stable Dependencies Principle, Stable Abstraction Principle

Stable Dependencies Principle (SDP)

Also Known As: N/A

Original Contributors: Robert C. Martin

Depend in the direction of stability.

The dependencies between packages in a design should be in the direction of the stability of the packages. A package should only depend upon packages that are more stable than itself.

A package is stable when it has a lot of incoming dependencies, as having many other packages depend on it is a definite way to make it difficult to change.

To illustrate this, the below example shows S, a stable package. Four other packages depend on S and therefore possibly four good reasons not to change. Package S is responsible to the four packages that depend on it. Also, S does not depend on anything which implies that there is no external influence to make it change, so S is independent.

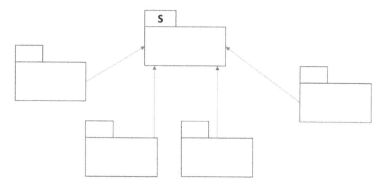

The below example shows X, an instable package. No packages depend on X, so it is irresponsible. X depends on four packages, so changes can potentially come from four external sources.

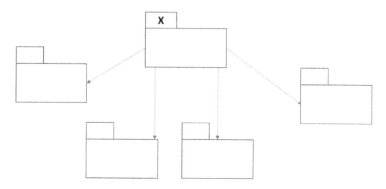

Instability I-Metric as defined below is used to measure the stability of a package.

Instability I=Ce/(Ca+Ce)

Ca = #of classes outside the package which depend on classes in the package (Afferent Coupling - incoming dependencies). Ce = #of classes outside the package which classes inside the package depend on (Efferent Coupling – outgoing dependencies). The I metric has the range [0, 1]. I = 0 indicates a highly stable package i.e.it is responsible and independent. I = 1 indicates a maximally instable package i.e. it is irresponsible and dependent.

To comply with this principle, the I metric of a package should be greater than the I metrics of the packages it depends on.

Quality Attributes Affected

Improves: Reusability

Reduces: Coupling

Metrics

Afferent Coupling, Efferent Coupling, Instability

Smells

Instable Packages

See Also

Minimize Coupling, Acyclic Dependencies Principle, Stable Abstraction Principle

The Stable Abstraction Principle (SAP)

Also Known As: N/A

Original Contributors: Robert C. Martin

A package should be as abstract as it as stable.

Stable packages are hard to change but they need not be hard to extend. Open Closed Principle suggests that a module can be extended without modifying it. Following that lead, this principle suggests that stable packages should be abstract to make it easy for extension. This principle is a corollary to Stable Dependency Principle.

Stable Dependency Principle and this principle combined together amount to Dependency Inversion Principle for packages. According to Stable Dependency Principle, dependencies should run in the direction of stability, and this principle says that stability implies abstraction. Hence dependencies should run in the direction of abstraction.

The below graphic representation provides a succinct summary of the approach to determine the usefulness and reusability of components. The abstractness and instability of a component should be balanced for a component to be useful and reusable. i.e. A component should be on the main sequence or closer to it.

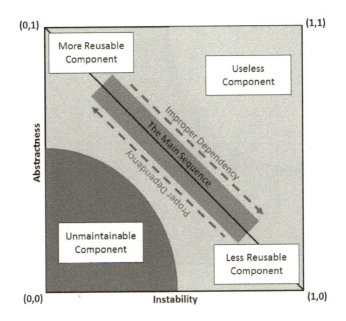

Quality Attributes Affected

Improves: Reusability and Maintainability

Reduces: Coupling

Metrics

Abstractness, Instability, Distance from the Main Sequence.

Smells

Concrete Package

See Also

Dependency Inversion Principle, Stable Dependency Principle, Open Closed Principle

134

General Principles

This section describes the following principles:

- Principles of Least Astonishment
- Law of Demeter
- Reuse Path Principle
- Documentation Principle

Principle of Least Astonishment (PLA)

Also Known As: Principle of Least Surprise

Original Contributors: M. F. Cowlishaw

> If a necessary feature has a high astonishment factor, it may be necessary to redesign the feature.

The principle can be restated as "User of a component should not be surprised by its behaviour" from software component design perspective. The easiest designs to use are those that demand the least new learning from the user. Usually a surprise is a side effect that goes beyond the scope of current abstraction level. It is often worth the extra effort and even compromising on aspects like performance to ensure the revised design is easy to use and does not surprise the users in any way. This way the design most effectively connects with the user's prior knowledge. Avoid playing tricks and excessive cleverness in interface design. A trivial example would be, if you are building a Calculator, add method should mean addition of numbers.

Quality Attributes Affected

Improves: Usability and Maintainability

Reduces: Complexity

Metrics

Astonishment Factor

Smells

Misleading Names, Unused Fields, Unused Parameters, Unused Methods, Unused Classes, Cryptic Error Messages

See Also

Abstraction, Maximize Cohesion

Law of Demeter (LOD)

Also Known As: Principle of Least Knowledge, Don't Talk to Strangers

Original Contributors: Ian Holland, Karl Lieberherr

Each unit should have only limited knowledge about other units: only units "closely" related to the current unit.
Or
Each unit should only talk to its friends; Don't talk to strangers.

Law of Demeter advocates structure shy style of design through restricting the kind of objects an object's method can call. According to this rule, an object's method should call methods from the following categories of objects only:

- The object itself
- The object's instance and class variables
- The method's parameters
- Any object the method creates
- Any object returned by a call to one of this object's methods

Notice that the list does not include objects that are returned by method calls to other objects. The below diagram illustrates a Client violating the Law of Demeter.

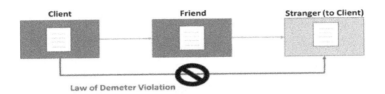

Law of Demeter Violation

Adherence to LoD does not mean "avoid chaining of calls". For example, you can chain calls when using the Builder pattern to construct complex objects without violating this law.

LoD promotes "Tell, don't ask" style, which leads to design that expresses intent at a high level of abstraction. The high level of abstraction makes the programs shorter and easier to maintain. This approach minimizes logical coupling but it does not address the physical aspects of coupling.

Quality Attributes Affected

Improves: Maintainability and Adaptability

Reduces: Coupling (logical)

Metrics

Demeter Distance

Smells

Method Chains, Anaemic Domain Model, Procedural Programming

See Also

Abstraction, Encapsulation, Tell Don't Ask, Minimize Coupling, Maximize Cohesion

Reuse Path Principle (RPP)

Also Known As: N/A

Original Contributors: Bertrand Meyer

> Be a reuse consumer before you try to be a reuse producer.

Reuse is the holy grail of software design and development. Every new paradigm includes reuse as a key reason why it needs to be adopted. The most common experience is that we don't see it working as promised. Reuse does not happen automatically. Not-Invented-Here syndrome could be hindering the reuse attitude among your team. You need to manage the reuse process to realize the promise. This principle provides the guideline that helps you to make reuse a priority.

A developer who reuses the work of other developers is called reuse consumer. A developer who creates reusable items is referred to as reuse producer. To promote reuse, you need to adopt "Reuse-First, build it only as a last resort" philosophy and have the necessary checks and balances in the development process.

Quality Attributes Affected

Improves: Reusability

Reduces: Duplication

Metrics

Number of Components Reused

Smells

Reinventing the Wheel, Not Invented Here syndrome

See Also

Documentation Principle

Documentation Principle (DOP)

Also Known As: N/A

Original Contributors: Bertrand Meyer

> Try to write the software so that it includes all the elements needed for its documentation, recognizable by the tools that are available to extract documentation elements automatically at various levels of abstraction.

A frequent problem with documentation is, it gets obsolete over time. It takes time and effort to keep the documentation up-to-date. Self-documentation is a way to address this issue effectively. The idea behind this principle is – make the software as self-documenting as possible. Most of the languages support documentation comments as part of source files recognized by tools to generate documentation automatically as part of the build process. We should leverage such features and use tools to generate documentation that provides various levels of details on design like, API Documentation, Class and Package Diagrams.

Quality Attributes Affected

Improves: Reusability and Maintainability

Reduces: Complexity

Metrics

Code vs Comment Density, Recency of Documentation, Traceability

Smells

Lack of Documentation, Obsolete Documentation

See Also

Reuse Path Principle, Manage Complexity

Appendix

References

Here is the list of books through which I came across many of the design principles.

- Structured Design: Fundamentals of a Discipline of Computer Program and Systems Design by Larry L. Constantine
- Design Patterns: Elements of Reusable Object-Oriented Software by Erich Gamma, Richard Helm, Ralph Johnson, John Vlissides
- Object-Oriented Software Construction by Bertrand Meyer
- Agile Software Development, Principles, Patterns, and Practices by Robert C. Martin
- Applying UML and Patterns: An Introduction to Object-Oriented Analysis and Design and Iterative Development by Craig Larman
- Design Patterns for Object-Oriented Software Development by Wolfgang Pree
- Smalltalk by Example: The Developers Guide by Alec Sharp
- The Pragmatic Programmer by Androw Hunt and Deve Thomas
- Fundamentals of Object-Oriented Design in UML by Meilir Page-Jones
- Object Models: Strategies, Patterns, and Applications by Peter Coad

The following books are good sources for understanding code and design smells.

- Refactoring: Improving the Design of Existing Code by Martin Fowler
- Refactoring for Software Design Smells: Managing Technical Debt by Girish Suryanarayana, Ganesh Samarthyam and Tushar Sharma

About the Author

Narayanan Jayaratchagan has more than 20 years of programming and software development experience. He has worked on various programming paradigms including Structured, Functional and Object-Oriented programming. He is passionate about researching software engineering literature. He finds it fascinating to explore the original sources and contributors of programming principles, patterns and best practices. He is an avid code reader. He explores the source code of JDK and other open source projects for pattern mining as a hobby.

www.ingramcontent.com/pod-product-compliance
Lightning Source LLC
Chambersburg PA
CBHW031241050326
40690CB00007B/901